I'm going sane one day at a time.

The Seven Shockras:

Birth

The family dance and no one knows the steps

Not all love is possible

Passion wanes

Carrot cake isn't a vegetable

Who I became

Dead is forever

Family...the scene of the crime.

Home is where the horror is.

Unchoose the Jews.

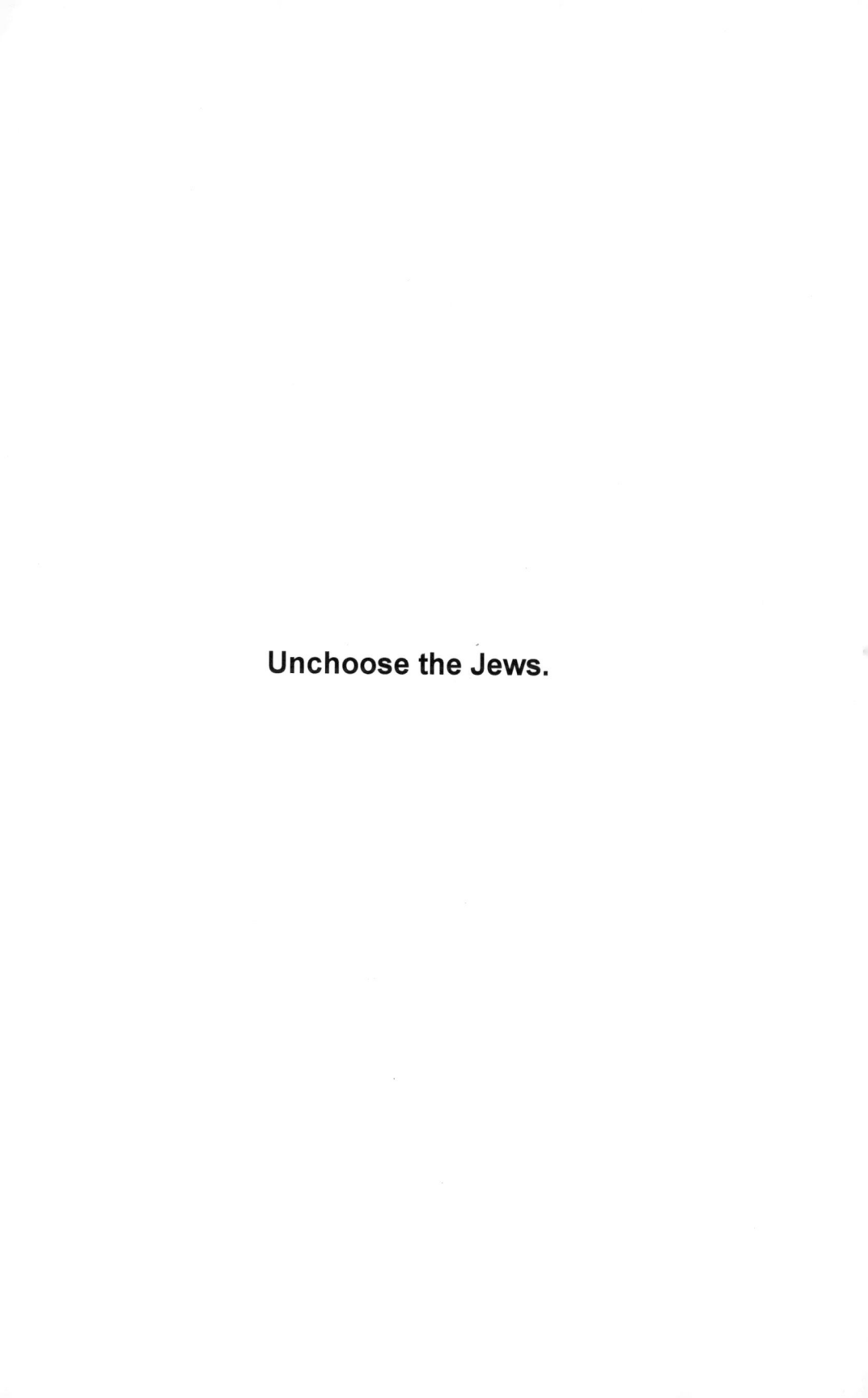

Treading water in the think tank!

I was a bed-wetter.

Grateful I wasn't a bed-shitter!

I thought all families have fart stories.

I'm out on a limb on the family tree.

Trauma queen!

I became my own mommy dearest.

Mortality Sighting!

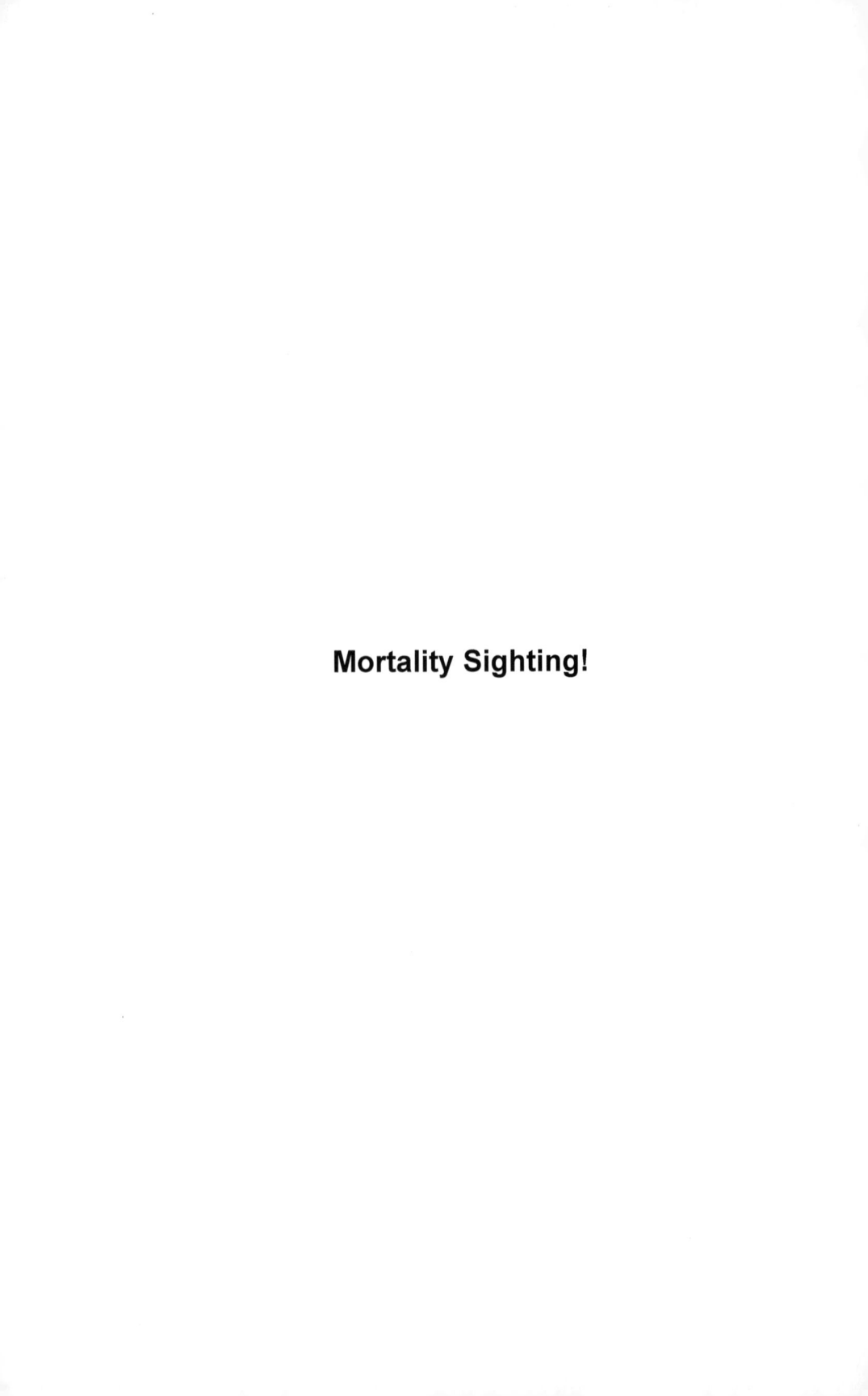

Existential terror...Have a great day!

Do your daily exorcise.

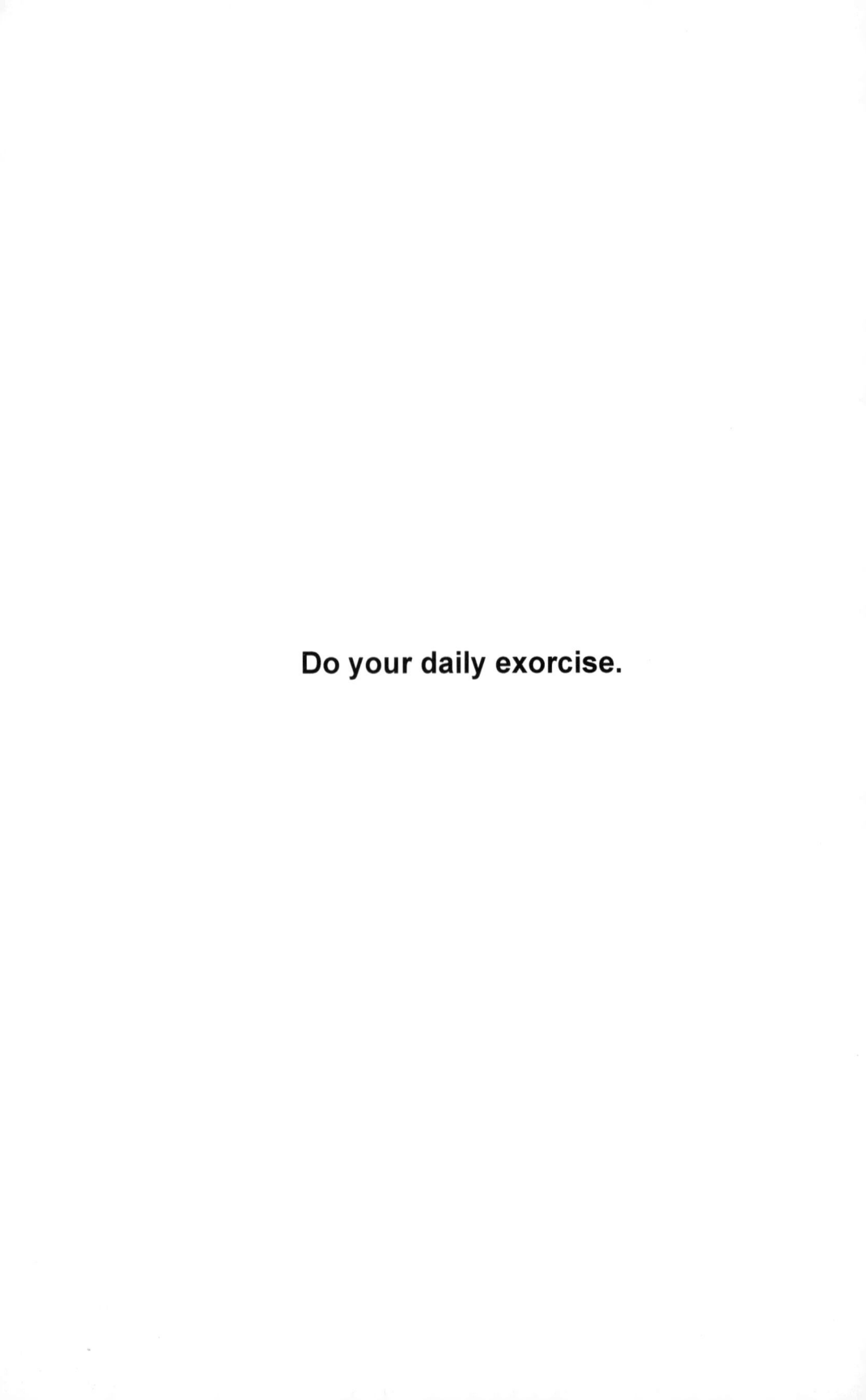

You hurt my feeling!

–Danny Louis

I've stopped rehearsing my death
as a New Year's resolution.

Not everything happens for a reason.

**I'm organizing the
CONTROL FREAK OLYMPICS.**

Alive in my tracks

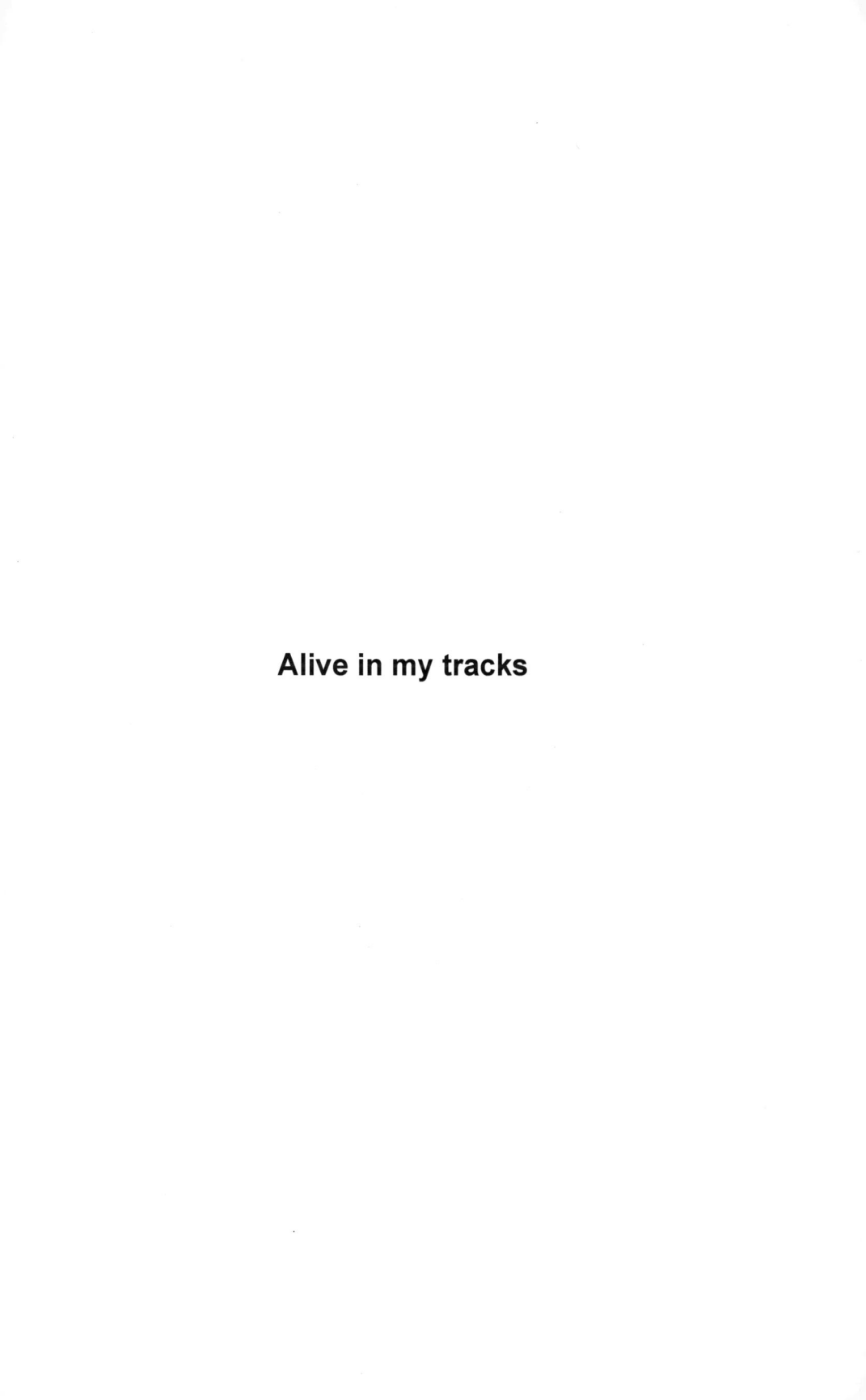

We are all in the middle of somewhere.

I can no longer die young.

One thing to cross off my anxiety list.

I used to think that what I said was what I meant...Ha!

If I'm thinking about peeing it's already too late!

I'm a thought magician.

I connect invisible dots,

spin out fantasy conclusions

and think they're real!

Welcome to the highlights of my low points.

Addiction - - as American as apple pie!

In Peru you would be tall.

–Roberto Guerra

I'm a hyper vigilante.

The thought police are after me!

MIND FIELD! Proceed with caution.

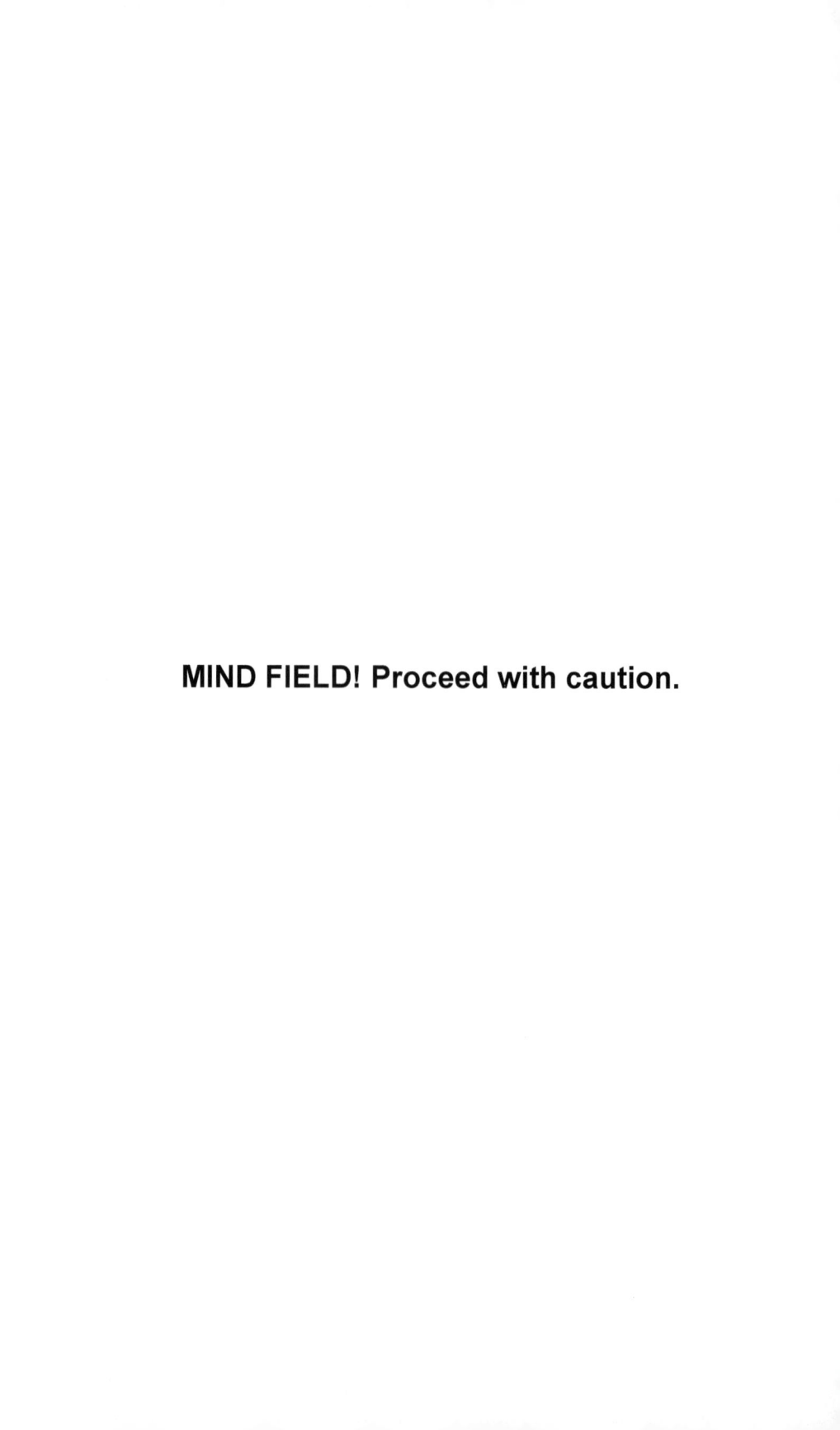

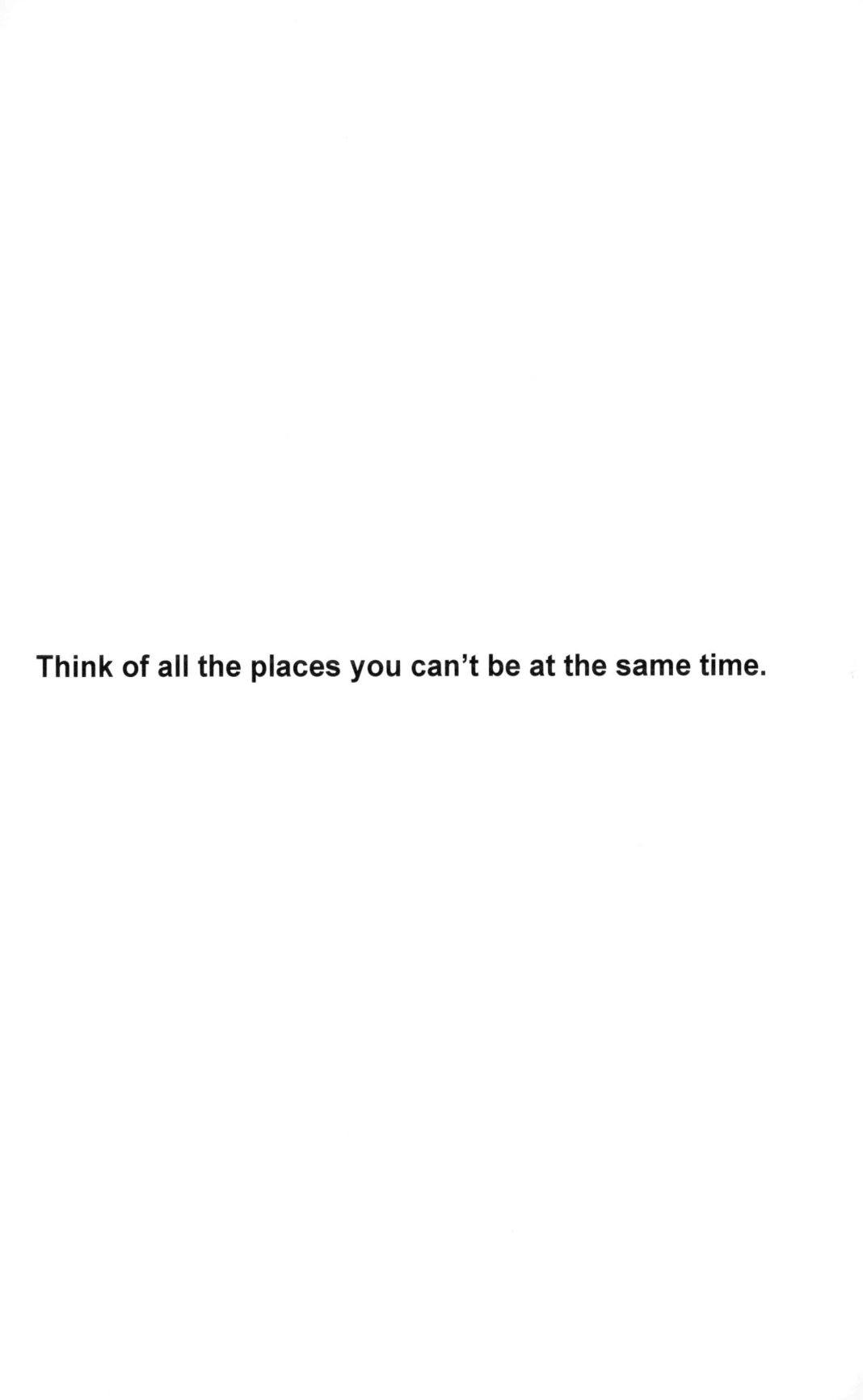

Think of all the places you can't be at the same time.

I find myself degriefing daily.

Addiction is an equal opportunity destroyer.

Daily I have to talk myself down from an emotional precipice.

You didn't have to be there.

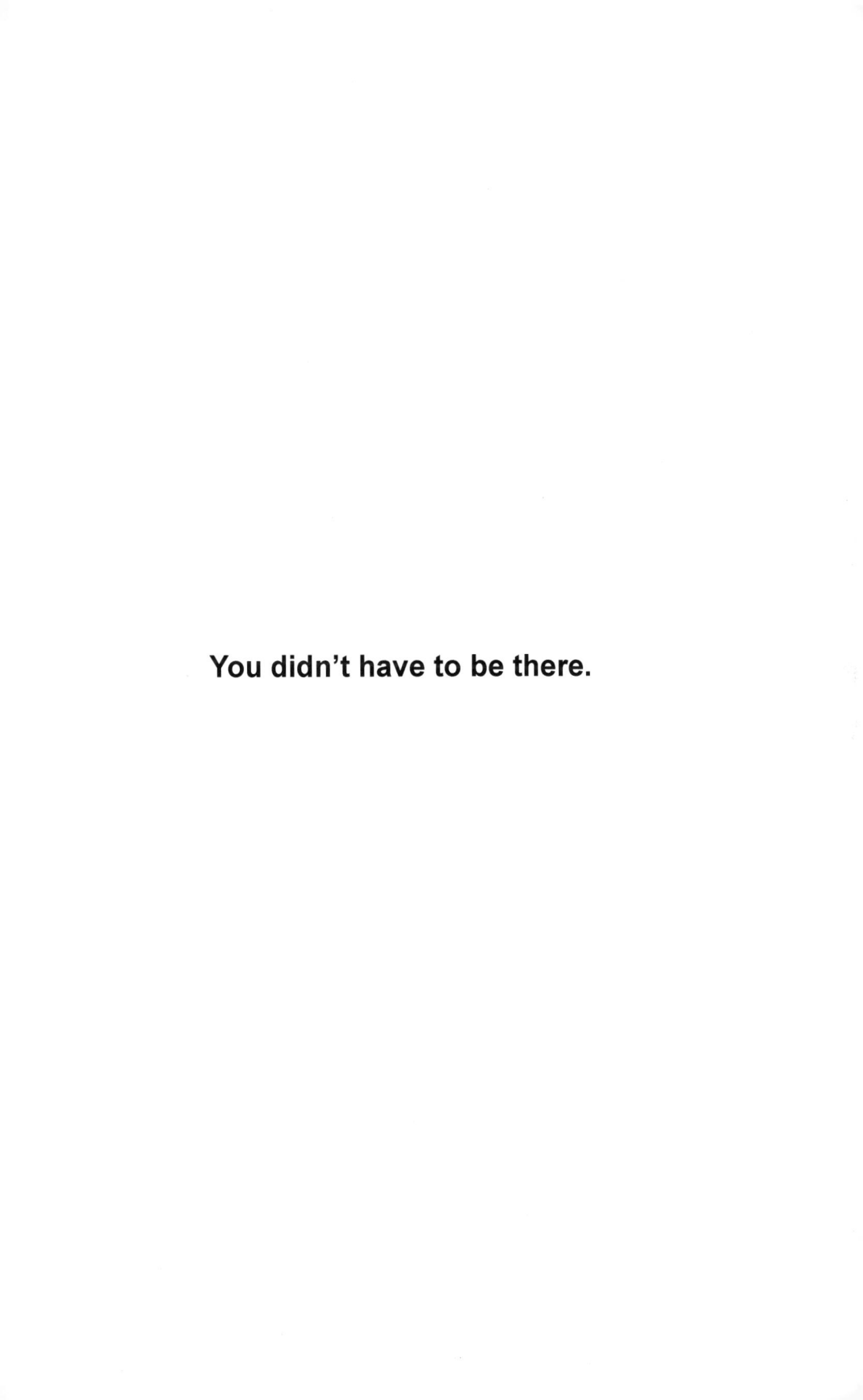

The past and the future are my specialty.

The present is the most illusive.

What about my inner adult?

—David Gillis

SELF Centered–the goal.

SELF absorbed, SELF obsessed...

now that's a problem!

Striving to be better than I really am.

I've lived long enough to have survived myself!

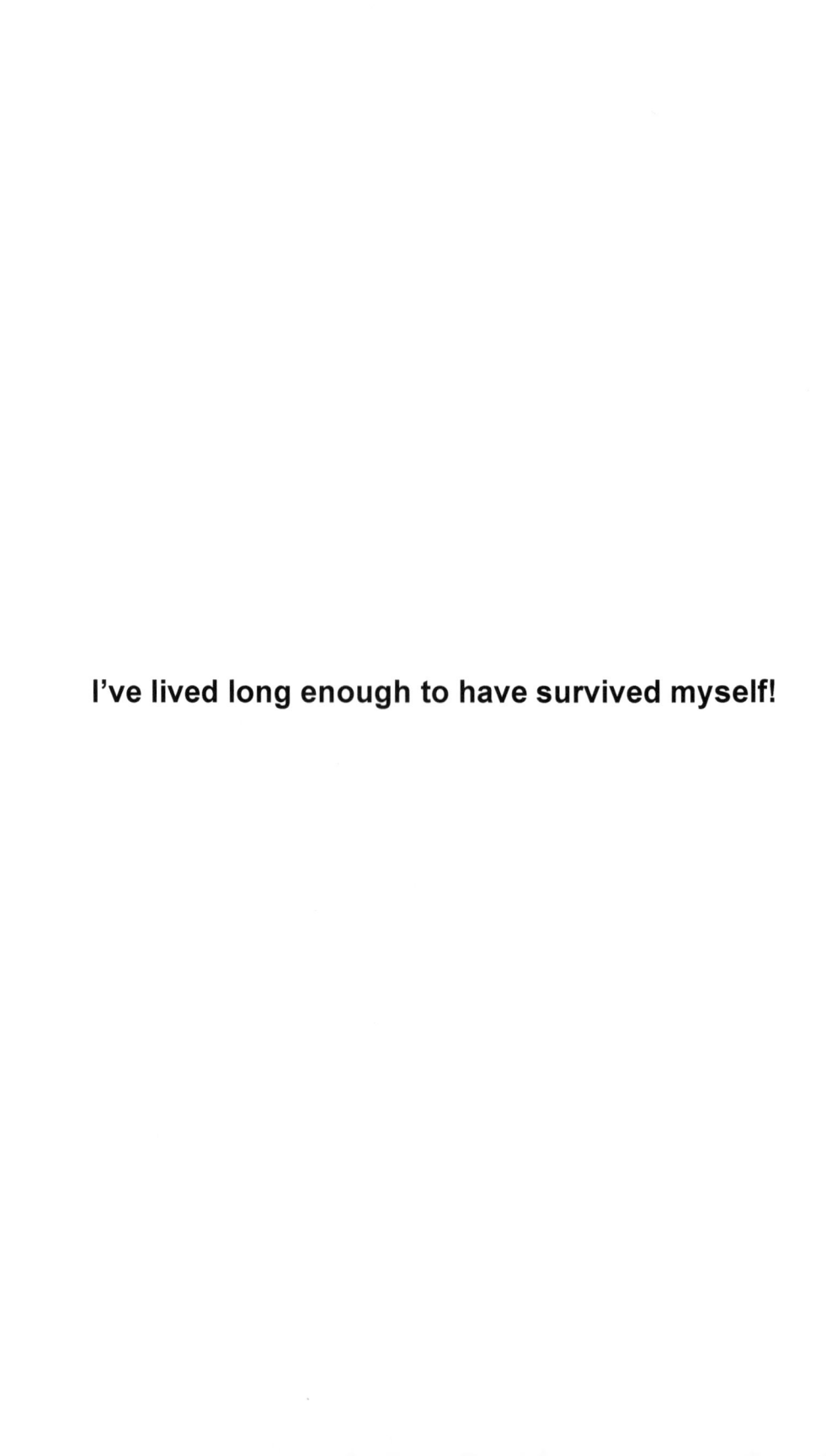

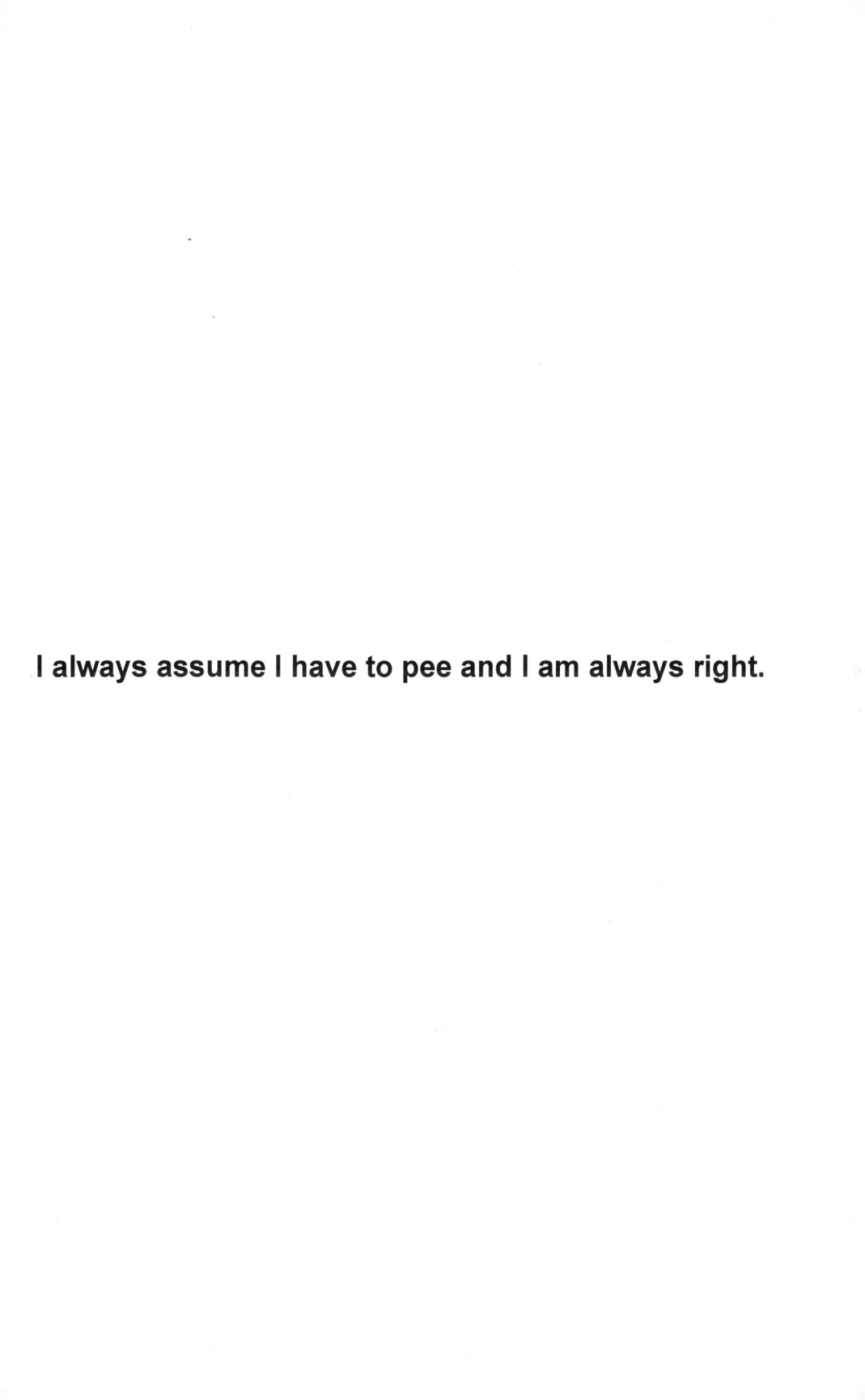

I always assume I have to pee and I am always right.

"FREE TO PEE, YOU AND ME"

(adult pads)

We are the olders. I'll toke to that.

Free Range Seniors

Get your tongue out of my ear!

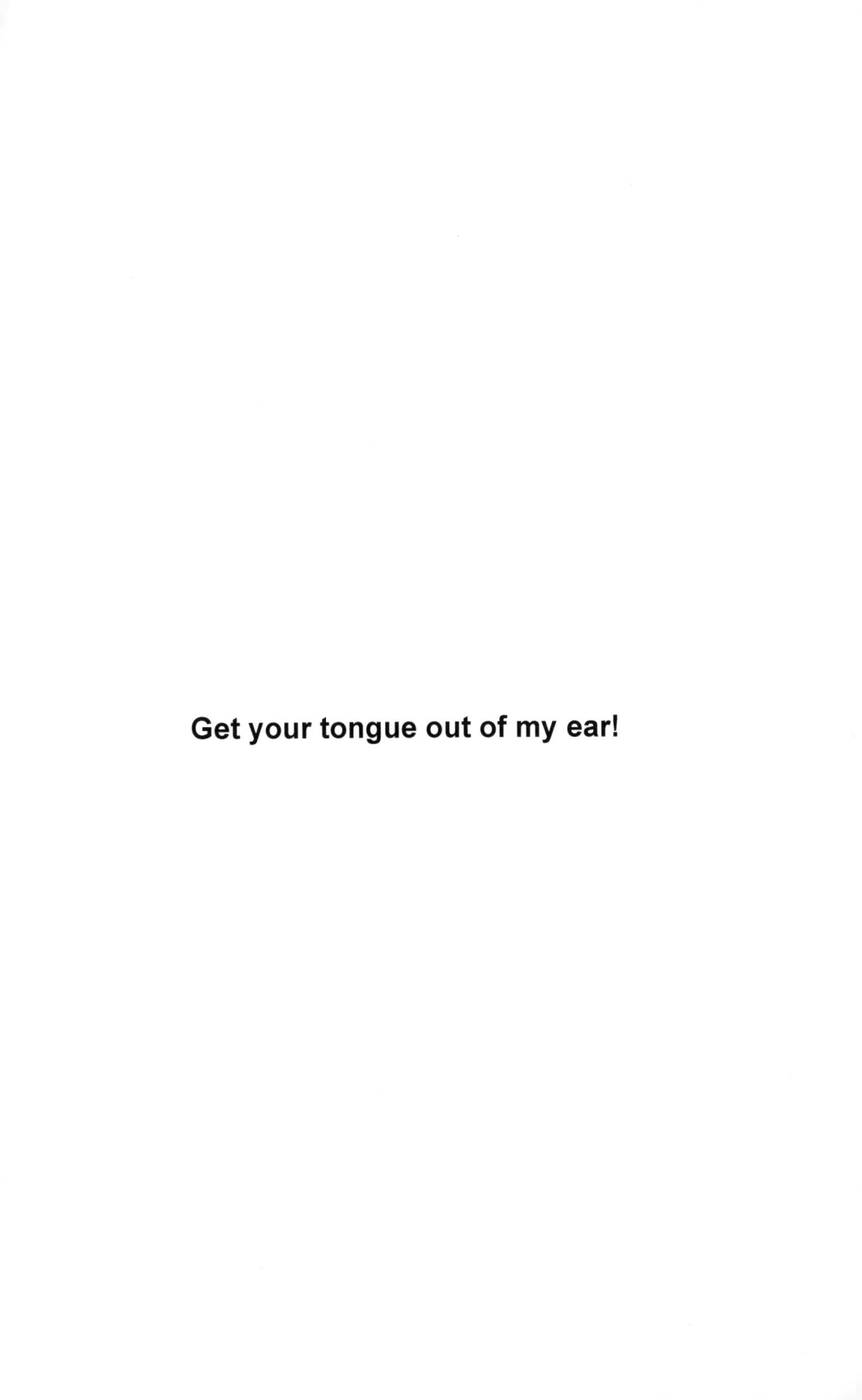

Where did my libido go?

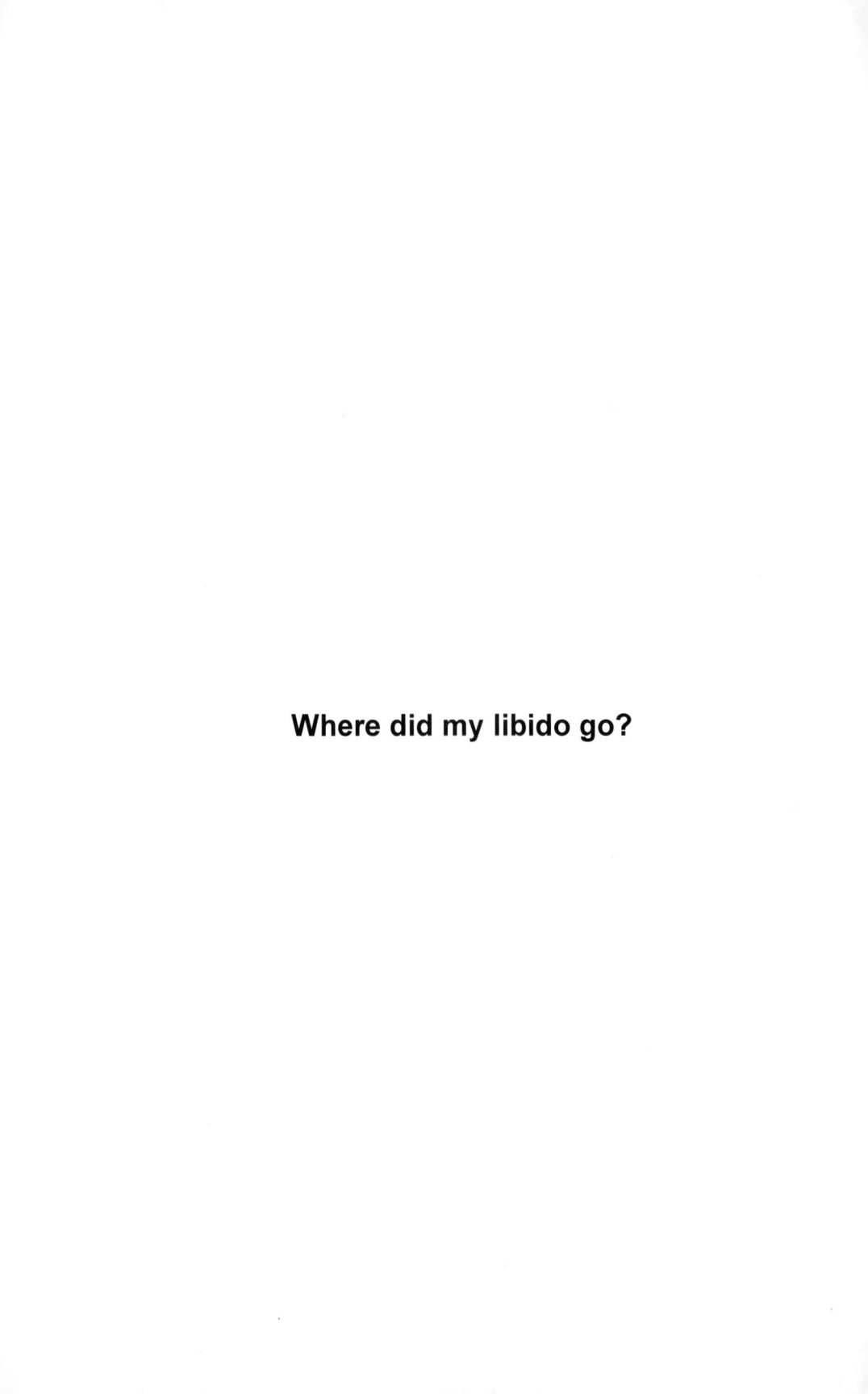

Dinner is earlier.

Early is earlier.

Late is earlier.

Shit is fertilizer.

Bolder and bolder,

shoulder to shoulder,

older and older!

What happened to the burning bush between my legs?

The bald eagle has landed.

Breathless...not a good idea.

Death has a life of its own.

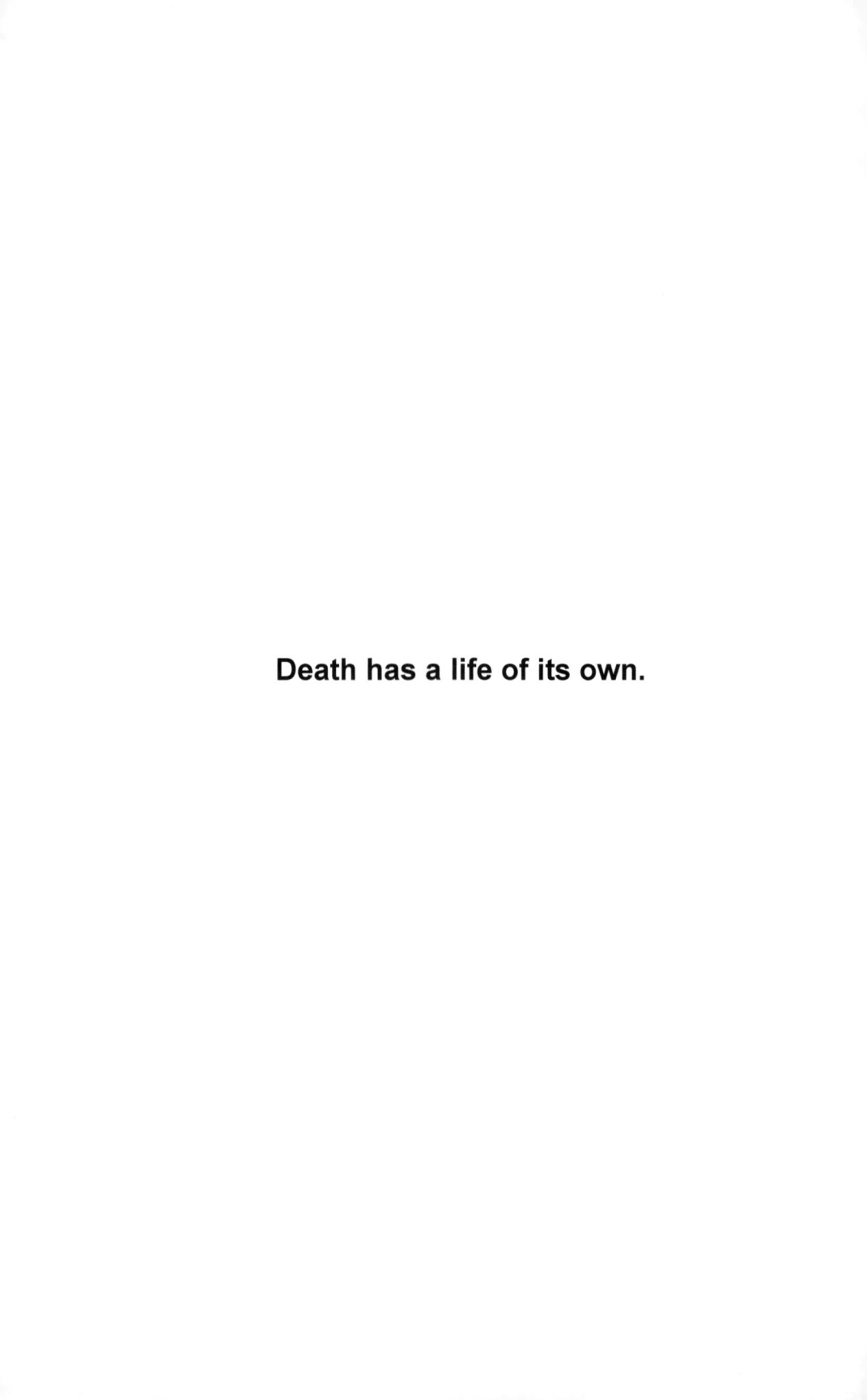

My segues are becoming confidential.

Welcome to the non-segue-tour.

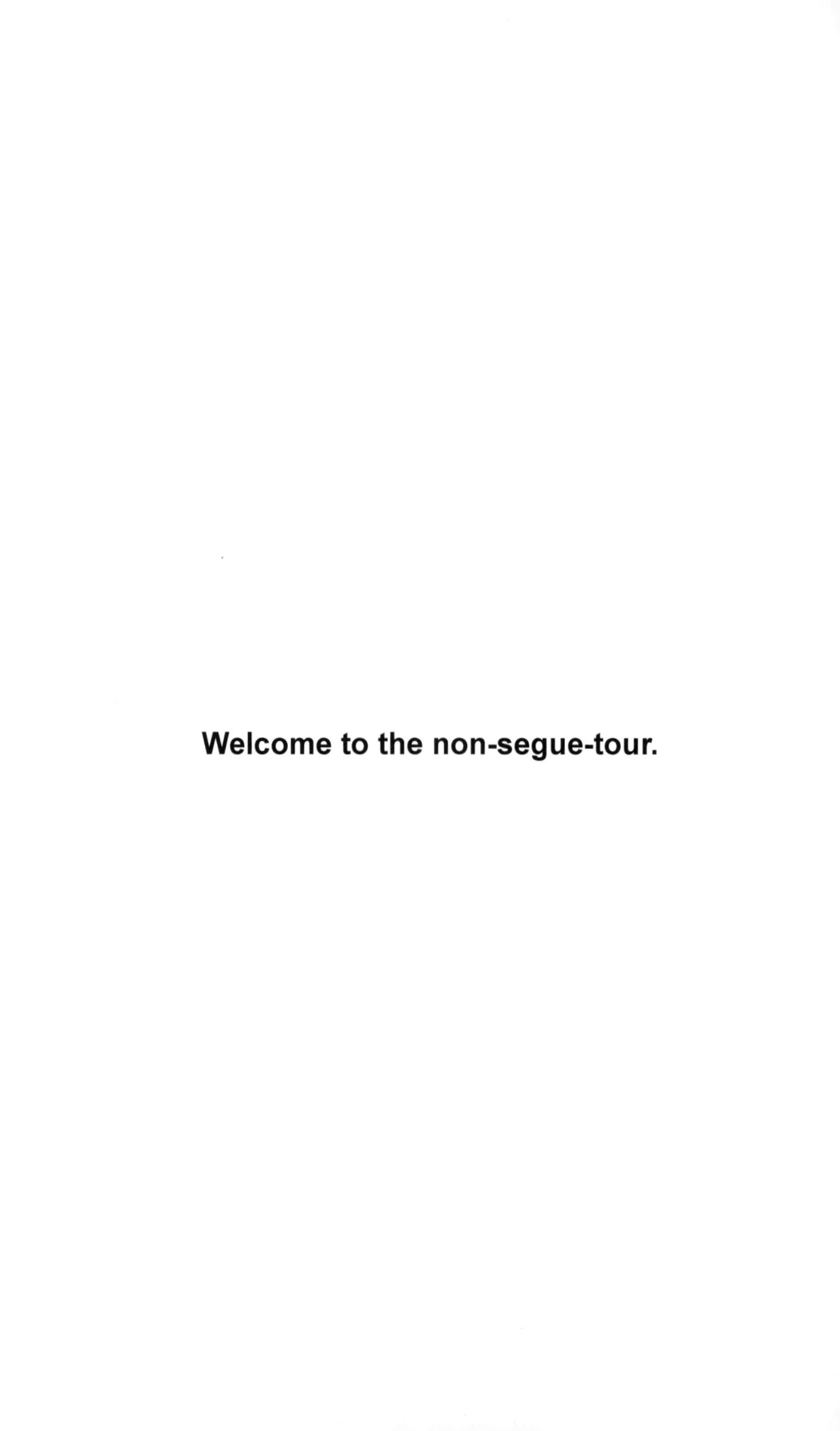

Only the lucky get to muddle.

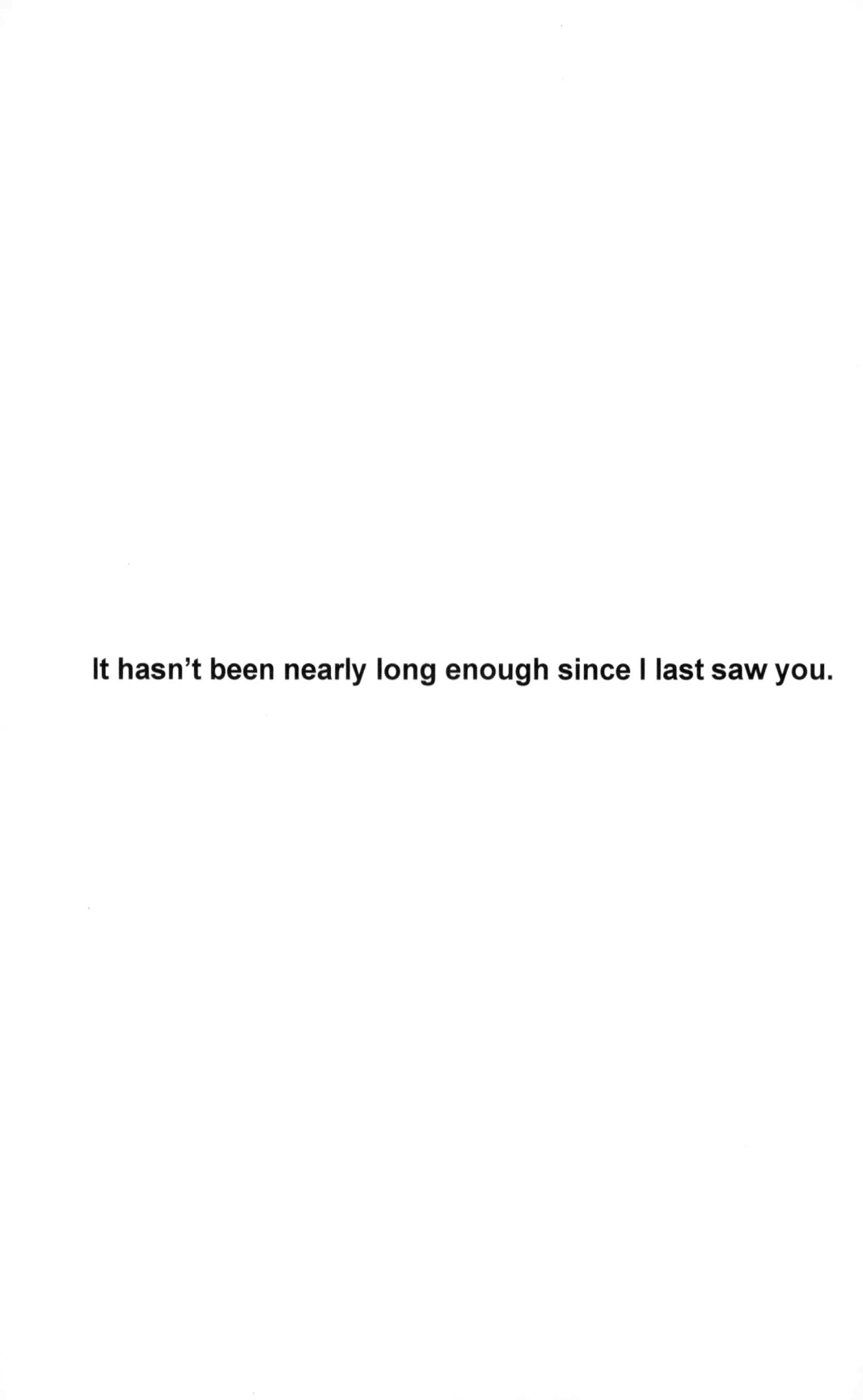

It hasn't been nearly long enough since I last saw you.

This is how I look.

This is my age.

I look my age.

Think outside the yurt!

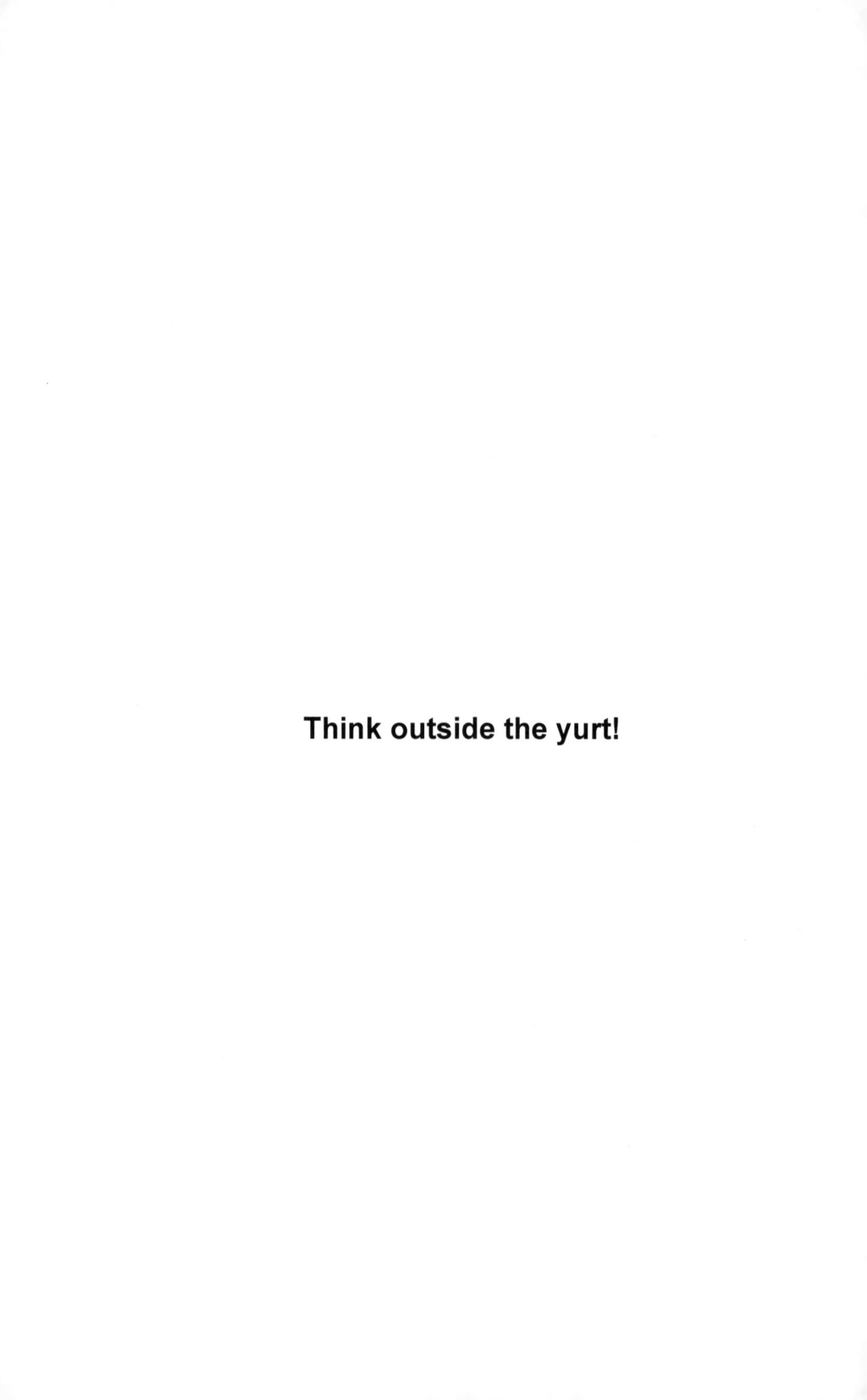

My new bra size is 36 long!
(not an original)

Carbs & weed are my proof of a higher power!

Mind altering? You bet!

Out of my mind? Good idea!

I don't get the munchies when I'm stoned.

I reserve domain names.

I own more than 20 domain names.

I need a younger dealer!

I'm with an older man.

I'm his older woman.

It's to live for.

I don't read as fast as I never did.

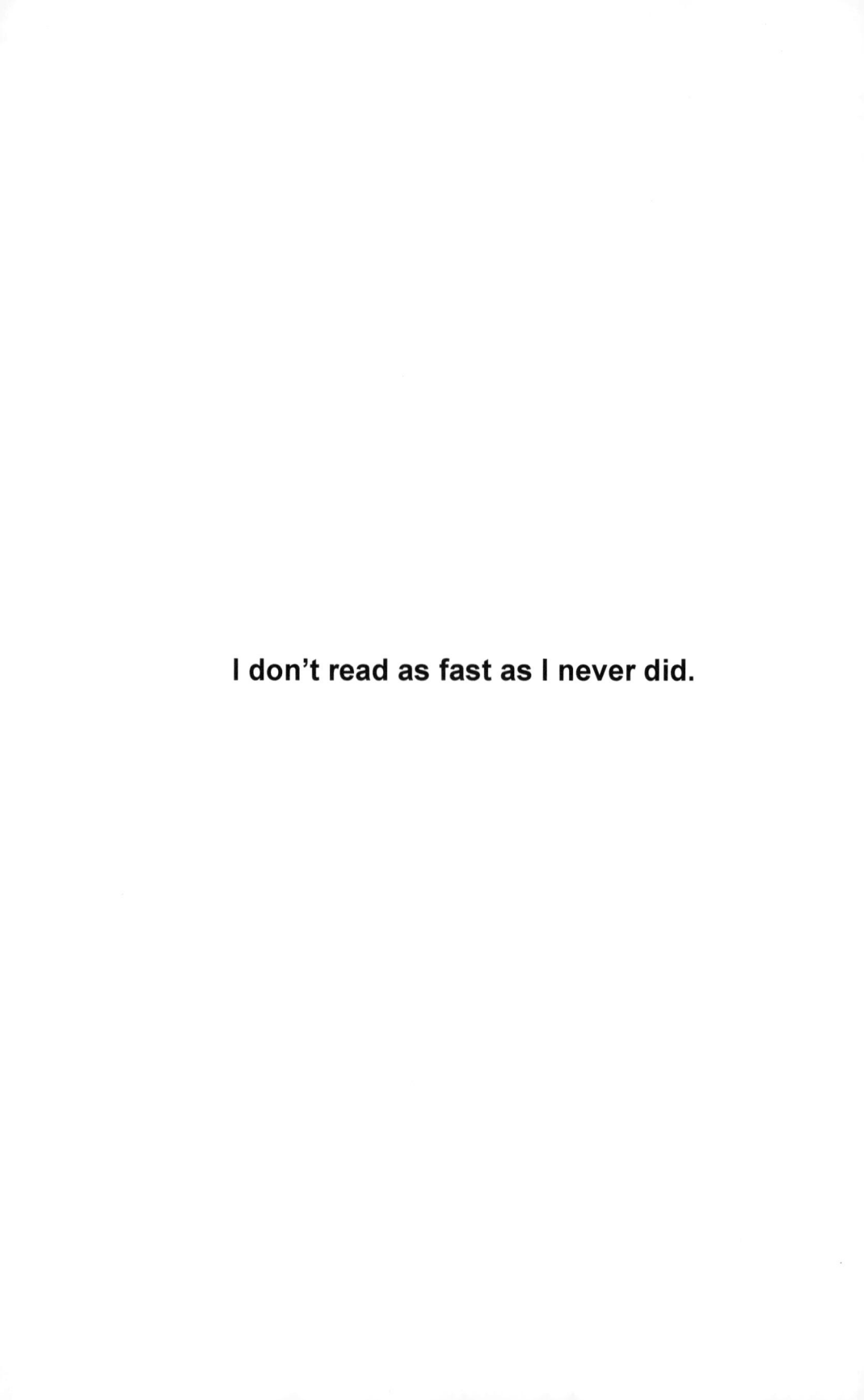

If we can't remember people,

at least they will always be new to us.

Remember 69?

You could choke!

Sixty is the new sixty.

Seventy is the new seventy.

I am constantly repsychling.

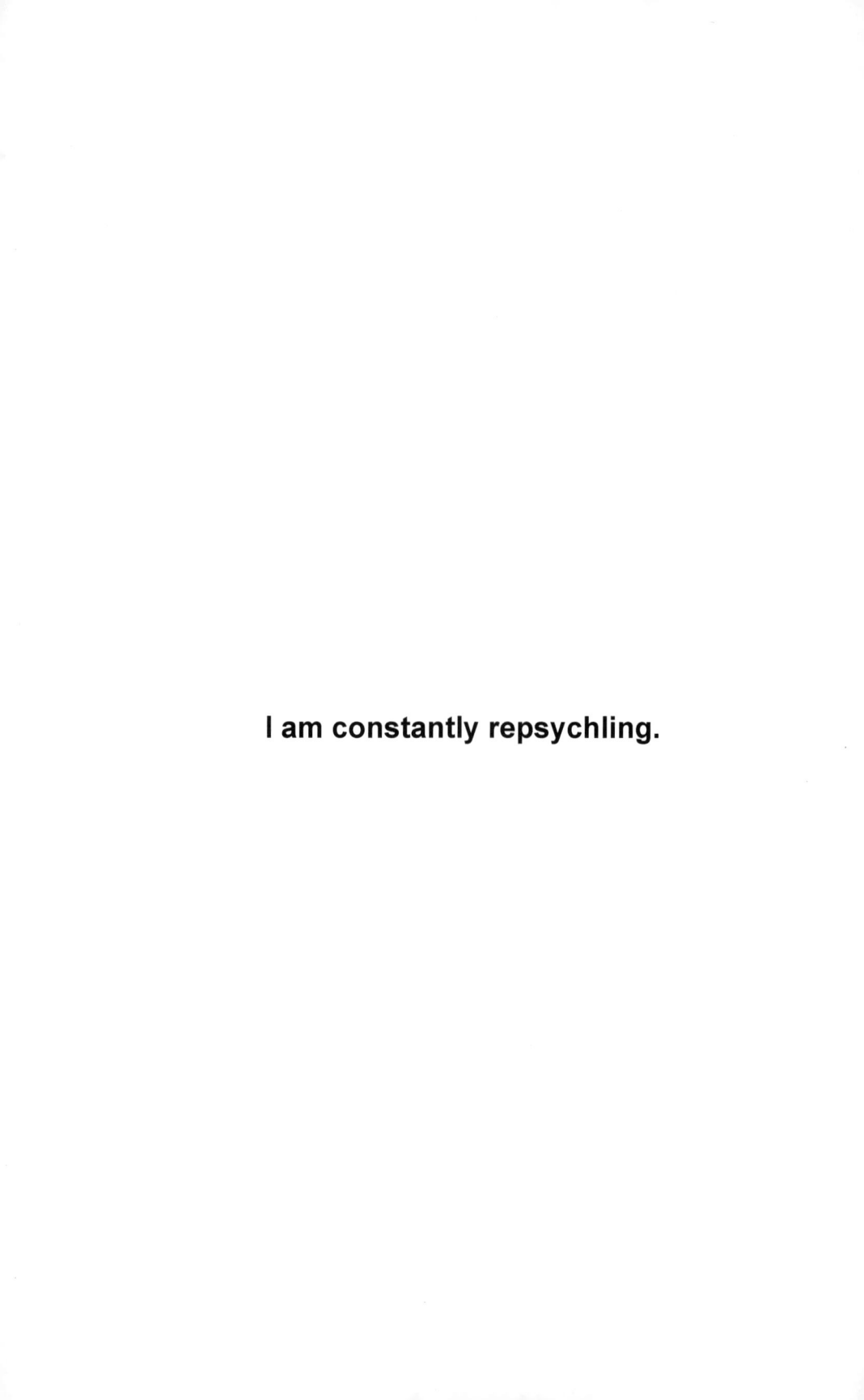

I live with a person who is another person!

And he has his own ideas!

I was not prepared for that.

I never left and now I'm back!

—Roswell Rudd

**The old demons retired to Florida

and didn't even say goodbye!**

I'm as grown up now as I'm going to be.

Joy is good! Who knew?

I will never not see it the same way again.

For my 70th birthday, I gave myself a surprise party.

Turning 70 is one big fucking surprise.

**One day the last thing I said
will be the last thing I say…
and vice versa**

The first hundred years are the hardest.

—Ivan Gillis

I put on and take off my retrospectacles.

Thank you to all the truly humorous people in my life. Too many to name so I will name and claim my most dear family starting with my mom and dad, Freda and Ivan, to my brother and sister David and Renee, my nephews Ivan, and Aram, my niece Sarah, and to the most recent generation of great nephews, Max and Jonah, and great niece Ezri.

We are funny and funny is good.

PUNishment reigned down on all of us and one of the sounds that filled the apartment was laughter.

If I can't laugh and don't want salad, then I know I am in deep shit!

Humor got me through and I highly recommend it as my favorite way to disassociate. Finding the humorous spin, giving it a good twirl and finally–FINALLY–being able to laugh at myself, to find the humor about myself, that was the real beginning of my writing.

Thank you my dear Roswell for filling my life with your magnificent sound and musical creations. You are an endless inspiration and game for all creative things, forever encouraging, generous and helpful. I know that living with me is another task that requires disassociation!

Thank you to to my friends Bonnie Anderson & Jocelyn Wills who laughed in all the right places–and some of the wrong places!

Thank you to friend Kathy Brew for her attention to detail, time devoted and excellent suggestions for change. Too many exclamation marks!!!

Thank you Kate McGhloughlin who is so funny and helps me , always with humor, take the high road.

Thank you to Eva Tenuto and TMI Project (tmiproject.org) for providing the unique setting to say things out loud, from page to stage; for insightful criticism and excellent editing that always makes it better.

Thank you to the multi-talented babe Julie Novak (julienovak.com) for her skills and patience. A star shines bright.